LITTLE HOUSE IN THE BIG WOODS

by
Laura Ingalls Wilder

Teacher Guide

Written by:
Phyllis A. Green

> ### Note
> The Harper Trophy paperback edition of the book was used to prepare this teacher guide. The page references may differ in the hardcover or other paperback editions.

ISBN 1-56137-030-4

To order, contact your local
school supply store, or—

Novel Units, Inc.
P.O. Box 791610
San Antonio, TX 78279

Table of Contents

Skills and Strategies

Listening/Speaking
Listening for details, sound
words, discussion,
interviewing

Comprehension
Predicting, sequencing,
comparison/contrast

Writing
Journaling, descriptive,
narrative, diary, letter-writing

Thinking
Sorting, visualizing, research

Vocabulary
Multiple meanings, word
mapping

Literary Elements
Similes, metaphors, story
elements, personification,
hyperbole, characterization

Summary

Beloved since being published in 1932, *Little House in the Big Woods*, tells of the author's childhood in a log cabin in Wisconsin. Laura's remembrances start out, "Once upon a time" and continue as from a child's view in telling about her life as a five-year-old. A full year is detailed and gives the reader a warm poignant glimpse into wilderness life in the nineteenth century. Always pleasantly upbeat, the tale focuses on survival of the family of five—providing food, shelter, safety, and emotional support to each other.

About the Author

Laura Ingalls Wilder was born in 1867 in Wisconsin. Her "Little House" books detail her family's pioneering experiences as the family moved from Wisconsin through Kansas, Minnesota, Iowa, and the Dakota Territory. After marrying Almanzo Wilder in 1885, she lived in Florida, Minnesota, and Missouri.

In 1932, when Wilder was 65, *Little House in the Big Woods* was published. Between 1932 and 1943, eight "Little House" books were written while Laura was living at Rocky Ridge Farm. Laura and Almanzo celebrated their 50th wedding anniversary in 1935. Laura Ingalls Wilder died in 1957.

The Little House stories were adapted for a television series, "Little House on the Prairie" and a Broadway musical, "Prairie."

Other Children's Books by Laura Ingalls Wilder

By the Shores of Silver Lake
The Long Winter
Little House in the Ozarks
Little House on the Prairie
Little Town on the Prairie
On the Banks of Plum Creek
These Happy Golden Years

Procedure for Teaching the Novel

The novel will be read one chapter at a time, using DRTA (Directed Reading Thinking Activity) method. This technique involves reading a section, predicting what will happen next (making good guesses) based on what has already occurred in the story. The children continue to read and everyone verifies the predictions. (See pages 7-8 of this guide.)

Initiating Activities

(Teacher may choose among the suggestions.)

1. Visit a historic log cabin as a field trip, build a Lincoln Logs cabin, or look at log cabin pictures and construction. What would life be like if you lived in a log cabin? Make a predictions chart.

2. The time of the book is more than 100 years ago. What "modern inventions" would have been missing from the life of those in the book? Generate a class list. *(telephone, electricity, cars, paved roads, photocopying)*

3. Interview older children who enjoyed the television program, "Little House on the Prairie." Why did you like it? What kind of plots did the show have? Tell us about the characters.

4. Read aloud the beginning of the story. Ask students to listen for details. Perhaps then allow them to see the individual books to verify details. Start a class mural to depict the setting and incidents retold in the book.

5. Display these items (photograph, models, etc.) which will be found in the book. Identify and then predict: trundle bed, panther, muskrats, corn cob doll, wolves, smoke house (see page 8 in the book), otter.

6. Where is the little house in the Big Woods? *(Pepin County, Wisconsin)* Locate on a map. (See page 9 for map.)

Vocabulary Activities

Overview: We suggest that a portion of the reading instructional time daily be used for vocabulary work, varying between individual, small group, and whole class activities.

1. Make a dictionary with meanings of the words or pictionary with pictures drawn to identify the words.

2. Student chooses (or is given) a word to compose an advertisement to "sell" his word.

3. Student sorts the vocabulary words according to part of speech (describers, names, actions).

4. Be a detective. Teacher writes a definition on the board. Students match with their individual vocabulary words.

5. Provide short phrases to explain selected vocabulary words as to an alien who has come to earth and wants to explain words and objects in an intergalactic museum. For example: a "bridge" would be "road over water."

6. Connect 2 or 3 of the vocabulary words. From a list of words, the student chooses 2 or 3 to connect and explain. For example, in Chapter One, "Muskrat and mink go together because they are both small animals that can be trapped for their furs." Here's the pattern: _____ and _____ go together because _____.

7. Use some of the words in figurative language.

   Similes are comparisons using "like" or "as."

   Metaphors are comparisons without like or as.

   Personification gives human traits and mannerisms to inanimate objects.

   Hyperbole is extreme exaggeration.

8. Create an attribute web or other word map for pioneer words and descriptions from the book. Sorting and classifying is encouraged.

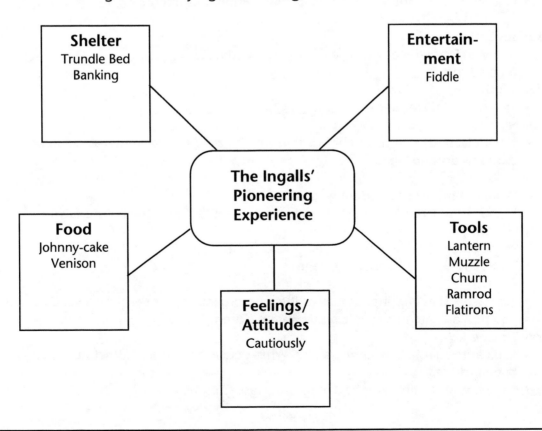

Journal Prompts

Overview: While studying the book, you are encouraged to provide journal time for students to write. Here are some possible prompts.

Chapter One:
- Describe your own "best of all time."
- What is a Big Woods?

Chapter Two:
- How has "woman's work" (homemaking) changed since the time of the book?
- How would your family cope if you lived in a little house in a big woods 100 years ago?

Chapter Three:
- What are some of the most common morals and advice that parents give to their children?
- What makes familiar places different and scarier after dark?

Chapter Four:
- How has whittling changed in the last 100 years?
- Dogs really do act as guardians for their owners. Agree or disagree and defend your answer.

Chapter Five:
- How are your Sundays similar to or different from the Ingalls?
- Times have surely changed since the time depicted in this book. Discuss.

Chapter Six:
- Illusion is important to the stories in this chapter. Comment.
- Spring is best in the anticipation.

Chapter Seven:
- Many childhood memories deal with food and tastes.
- Maple syrup is _____.

Chapter Eight:
- Family parties are special because _____.

Chapter Nine:
- What places do you remember visiting which gave you many interesting images (as the town did for Mary and Laura)?

Chapter Ten:
- What are the sounds and songs of summer?
- Why is summertime so much work for the Ingalls? What is the nature of your summers?

Chapter Eleven:
- What parenting advice would you give Uncle Henry and Aunt Polly?
- What advice would you give Charley?

Chapter Twelve:
- Teamwork is as important today as it was in organizing for the threshers. Comment.
- Squirrels are interesting animals to watch. Comment.

Chapter Thirteen:
- Look at the illustration on page 229. What details do you see? What other details might have been included?
- Now is now. It can never be a long time ago. Comment.

Using Predictions in the Novel Unit Approach

We all make predictions as we read—little guesses about what will happen next, how the conflict will be resolved, which details given by the author will be important to the plot, which details will help to fill in our sense of a character. Students should be encouraged to predict, to make sensible guesses. As students work on predictions, these discussion questions can be used to guide them: What are some of the ways to predict? What is the process of a sophisticated reader's thinking and predicting? What clues does an author give us to help us in making our predictions? Why are some predictions more likely than others?

A predicting chart is for students to record their predictions. As each subsequent chapter is discussed, you can review and correct previous predictions. This procedure serves to focus on predictions and to review the stories.

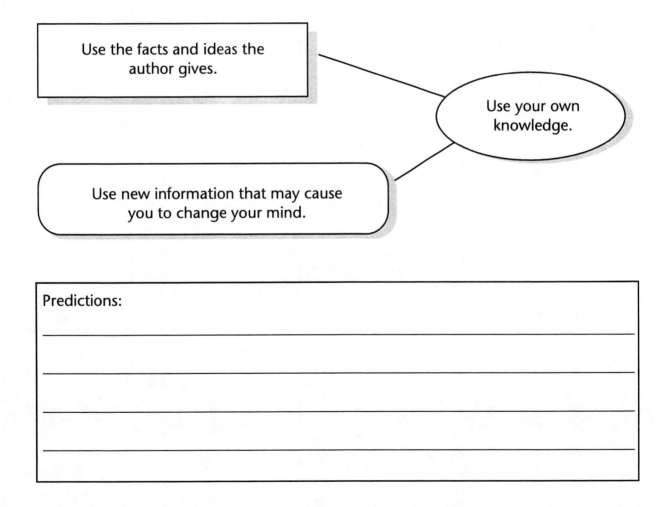

Use the facts and ideas the author gives.

Use your own knowledge.

Use new information that may cause you to change your mind.

Predictions:

_____

_____

_____

_____

Prediction Chart

What characters have we met so far?	What is the conflict in the story?	What are your predictions?	Why did you make those predictions?

United States Map

Chapter One: "Little House in the Big Woods"   Pages 1-23

Plot Summary
Laura introduces the little log house in the Big Woods. The family prepares for winter.

Vocabulary

muskrats 2	mink 2	otter 2	wagon track 2
venison 5	hinges 6	hickory 7	smoldered 7
pantry 12	cautiously 13	cracklings 17	johnny-cake 17
pot-liquor 17			

Discussion Questions and Activities

1. What is the setting of the story? *(Wisconsin log cabin in the Big Woods in 1872)*

2. How did the family prepare for winter? *(They shoot a deer, smoke meat, salt meat, salt fish, slaughter a pig, tie onions into log ropes, hang peppers on threads in the attic, pile pumpkins and squashes in the attic, store yellow cheeses on the pantry shelves, and dry herbs for medicine in the attic.)* How do you prepare for winter? Compare on a T-diagram.

    Suggested answers only (accept variations).

Your Preparations	Ingalls' Preparations
•Storm windows	
•Weatherstripping	
•Get out winter clothes	
•Find mittens	
•Buy new boots	
•New winter jackets	

3. What playthings did Laura and Mary have? *(dolls, pig bladder ball, squashes and pumpkins to play house)*

4. Why did the author say, "The best times of all were at night"? *(page 20, warm, cozy, needs were met, etc.)*

Supplementary Activities

1. Compare your home to Laura's. (See T-diagram on next page.)

Your Home	Laura's
	•*Log cabin* •*Wisconsin* •*Trees all around* •*No other houses nearby*

2. Writing: Laura's house is the little house in the Big Woods. What would you call your house if you were writing a book? your best friend's house? your grandparents' house?

3. Classifying: Start a listing of the foods mentioned in the book. Begin thinking of what you could have at a finale party when you finish the book. Which of the foods on your list have you eaten?

4. Start a class mural of the setting in the book. The mural will be a whole class cooperative effort including illustrations and narrative descriptions.

Chapter 2: "Winter Days and Winter Nights"   Pages 24-44

Plot Summary
Laura describes winter. Pa tells "The story of Grandpa and the Panther."

Vocabulary

panes 26	trundle bed 28	churn-dash 31	churn 31
scramble 36	brindle 38		

Discussion Questions and Activities
1. How did the Ingalls spend winter days?

Pa	Ma	Laura and Mary
•*Checking his trap line* •*Hunting*	•*Wash on Monday* •*Iron on Tuesday* •*Mend on Wednesday* •*Churn on Thursday* •*Clean on Friday* •*Bake on Saturday* •*Rest on Sunday*	•*Help Ma with chores* •*Wipe dishes* •*Make beds* •*Make frost pictures*

2. How did the Ingalls spend winter nights?

Pa	Ma	Laura and Mary
•*Playing "mad dog"* •*Fiddling* •*Telling stories*	•*Rocking* •*Sitting by the fire*	•*Playing "mad dog"* •*Singing*

3. How does your family spend their winter days and nights? Compare to the Ingalls.

4. What was "The Story of Grandpa and the Panther"? (*A panther chased Grandpa atop his horse through the woods. Arriving home, Grandpa used his shotgun to kill the panther, which had leaped atop the horse.*)

Supplementary Activities

1. Interviewing: Interview a grandparent or parent. Tell them about "The Story of Grandpa and the Panther." Ask them to tell you of any family stories they might know. Share the stories with your classmates. Why are these stories special?

2. Research: What are the usual winter temperatures in the Big Woods in Wisconsin? What will you need to know to look for the answer? (*location of Big Woods in Wisconsin*) What references might you use?

3. Churn butter (shake heavy cream in a glass jar with each child taking a turn).

4. Storytelling: This book uses a storytelling manner, as well as several shorter stories within some chapters (like Grandpa and the Panther). Try class storytelling. Seat the class in a circle. The first person starts the story, continues for 30 seconds to a minute, and the next person continues all around the circle. Emphasize the story map components and the need for a conflict and its resolution.

Chapter 3: "The Long Rifle"   Pages 45-58

Plot Summary
Laura describes Pa's care of his rifle. The girls request telling of "The Story of Pa and the Voice in the Woods."

Vocabulary

buckskin 46	ramrod 47	gunstock 48	muzzle 49
powder horn 51	scurrying 54	ravines 55	briars 55
thrashing 58			

Discussion Questions and Activities

1. What was Pa's process for making bullets and cleaning his gun? *(He melts bits of lead in a big spoon, pours them into bullet-mold, waits one minute, and drops out a new bullet. Once the bullets are cooled, he trims lumps left by the hold in the mold. To clean gun, he pours boiling water into gun barrel and rubs up and down with ramrod until water runs clear. Then he greases inside of gun with greased rag on the ramrod. Next he rubs the outside of the gun. Then he rubs and polishes the gunstock.)* Why did Pa do the cleaning every night? *(Pa hunted every day and wanted to be sure the gun was ready.)* Are there any tools your father uses for his work which need to be "serviced" every night?

2. Why did Pa reload his gun after the daily cleaning? *(So the gun would be ready if needed. The Big Woods had many dangers and a gun could help.)*

3. Retell "The Story of Pa and the Voice in the Woods." *(pages 53-58)* What was the moral of the story? *(There's a good reason for the things parents tell their children.)* Do all stories have morals? Share other stories you know that have morals.

Supplementary Activities

1. Attribute Webs: You are beginning to know the characters in the story. Start an attribute web for Pa. (See pages 14-16 of this guide.)

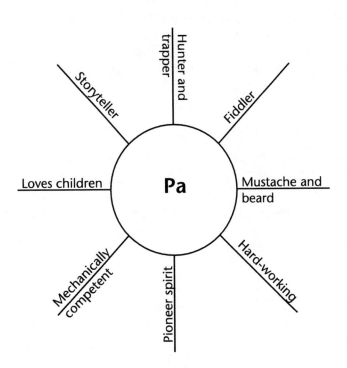

Using Character Webs—In the Novel Unit Approach

Attribute Webs are simply a visual representation of a character from the novel. They provide a systematic way for the students to organize and recap the information they have about a particular character. Attribute webs may be used after reading the novel to recapitulate information about a particular character or completed gradually as information unfolds, done individually, or finished as a group project.

One type of character attribute web uses these divisions:

• How a character acts and feels. (How does the character feel in this picture? How would you feel if this happened to you? How do you think the character feels?)

• How a character looks. (Close your eyes and picture the character. Describe him to me.)

• Where a character lives. (Where and when does the character live?)

• How others feel about the character. (How does another specific character feel about our character?)

In group discussion about the student attribute webs and specific characters, the teacher can ask for backup proof from the novel. You can also include inferential thinking.

Attribute webs need not be confined to characters. They may also be used to organize information about a concept, object or place.

Attribute Web

The attribute web below is designed to help you gather clues the author provides about what a character is like. Fill in the blanks with words and phrases which tell how the character acts and looks, as well as what the character says and what others say about him or her.

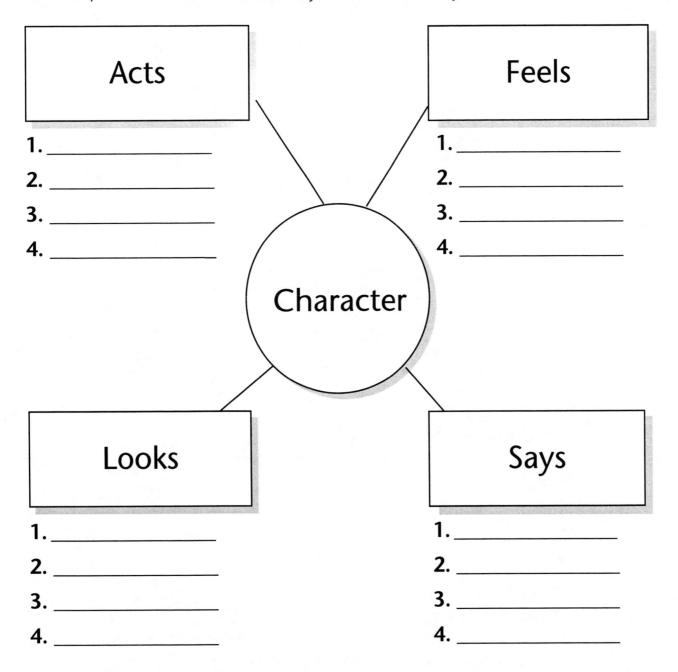

Acts
1. _____
2. _____
3. _____
4. _____

Feels
1. _____
2. _____
3. _____
4. _____

Character

Looks
1. _____
2. _____
3. _____
4. _____

Says
1. _____
2. _____
3. _____
4. _____

Attribute Web

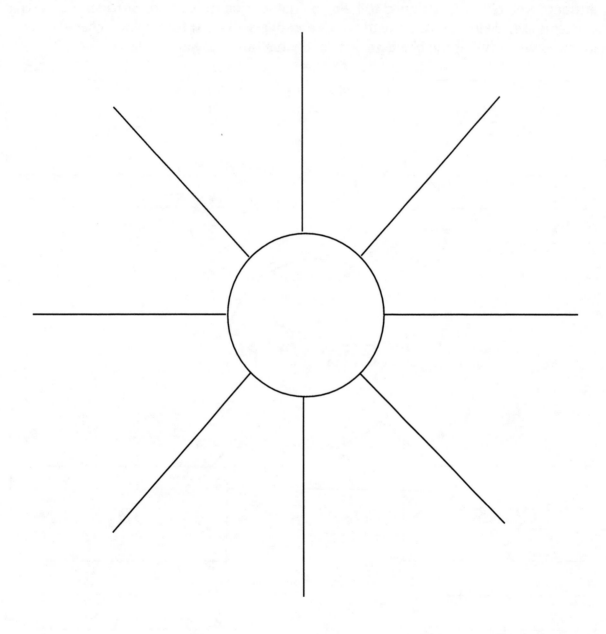

2. Writing: What sounds frighten you as the screech-owl frightened Pa? Write a short paragraph to answer.

3. Tell your parents or other adults the screech owl and panther stories. Ask them to tell you some stories of their own childhoods which the Wilder stories suggest to them. Share your findings with classmates and then create a class book to record the stories.

Chapter 4: "Christmas"   Pages 59-82

Plot Summary
The Ingalls prepare for a homespun, noncommercial Christmas. When Aunt Eliza and Uncle Peter arrive, they all hear about their dog's heroics in protecting Eliza from a panther.

Vocabulary

whittled 60	Swedish crackers 62	curlicues 63	squiggledy 63
ravine 68	snarled 69	savage 69	pokeberries 74
raveled 75	gaiters 77	flatirons 82	

Discussion Questions and Activities
1. How high was the snow in the beginning of Chapter 4 in feet and inches? Did the author tell you the answer directly? Can you figure out the answer? *(Page 59, The snow was "as high as Laura's head." Estimate how tall a typical five-year-old girl is.)*

2. How did the Ingalls celebrate Christmas? *(with a visit from Aunt Eliza, Uncle Peter, and the cousins)*

3. Compare how you play in the snow and how Laura, Mary, Peter, Alice, and Ella played in the snow. Use a Venn diagram.

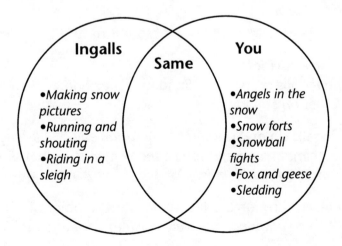

Ingalls / Same / You

•Making snow pictures
•Running and shouting
•Riding in a sleigh

•Angels in the snow
•Snow forts
•Snowball fights
•Fox and geese
•Sledding

4. What was Pa's Christmas present for Ma? *(a hand-carved shelf)*

5. How did Prince protect Aunt Eliza? *(The dog sensed danger from a panther at the spring and forced her to return to their house.)* Have you ever heard of a heroic dog? Share stories with the class.

6. What was Laura's special Christmas present? *(a rag doll)* Tell about a special present you've received.

7. Notice how all the chapters of the book have ended so far. What is the mood of the book?

Supplementary Activities
1. Prepare descriptions of favorite characters or scenes in the book. Read those descriptions to classmates who will try to identify them. Start with passages from this book. Extend with passages from other books.

2. Listen for details as the teacher or a classmate reads a favorite part of the story. After you've listened to the whole passage, with a partner, try to list the details. (Pages 60-63 with the Christmas preparations is one section filled with details.) Why do authors give details in such a passage?

3. Note the foods mentioned on page 62. Look for recipes in *The Little House Cookbook.*

Chapter 5: "Sundays"   Pages 83-100

Plot Summary
The Ingalls spruced up for Sundays which are quiet days with a religious focus. Laura remembers her sixth birthday.

Vocabulary
deserved 86   solemnly 88   catechism 91   cleft 97

Discussion Questions and Activities
1. How did all the Ingalls prepare for Sunday? *(They bathed on Saturday night and dressed in their best clothes on Sunday.)*

2. What did the Ingalls do on Sunday? *(They sat quietly and listened to Bible stories or The Wonders of the Animal World and sang Sunday hymns.)* What didn't the Ingalls girls do on Sunday? *(run, shout, or be noisy)*

3. Pa seemed to teach through stories. What was the point of "The Story of Grandpa's Sled and Pig"? *(Even grandparents were children once and had trouble not playing on Sundays.)*

4. How was Laura's sixth birthday like your birthdays? Describe the two birthdays on a T-diagram and then fill in a Venn Diagram.

My Birthday	Laura's Birthday
•*Birthday party* •*Presents* •*Birthday cake with candles* •*Happy Birthday is sung*	•*Five little birthday cakes* •*Happy Birthday was sung* •*"Pop Goes the Weasel" was played on the fiddle*

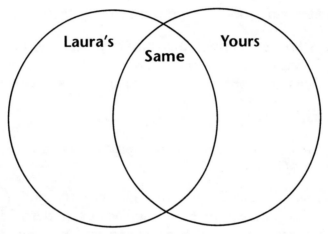

Supplementary Activities

1. Writing: Why are birthdays special? Write a short paragraph telling about your best birthday.

2. Review of the story so far: Use a story map to summarize the story through Chapter 5. (See page 30 of this guide.)

3. Art: Are there any items to be added to the class mural? Are there any details to be added which the author has now told us? *(Laura's new doll, provisions for winter, Ma's new Christmas shelf, etc.)*

4. Select a book character and keep a diary for a short length of time as that character might have done.

Chapter 6: "Two Big Bears"   Pages 101-116

Plot Summary
Spring in the Big Woods brings trading furs and bears coming out of their winter hibernation dens.

Vocabulary
trembling 101   lantern 103   calico 108

Discussion Questions and Activities

1. What were the signs of spring coming in the Big Woods? *(snow starting to thaw, icicles melting)*

2. Why didn't Pa take his gun when he went to town to trade his furs? *(Because there were too many furs.)* Was it a good idea to leave the gun at home? Why did it worry Ma?

3. What did Ma pat when Laura and she went to milk the cow? *(a bear)*

4. How did Ma reassure Laura about Sukey's safety after getting back into the cabin after seeing the bear? *(She pointed out the big, heavy logs in the walls. She hugged Laura.)* Why is reassurance important for children? How do your parents reassure you?

5. Look for these sentences on page 107.

   "All around the house the wind went crying as though it were lost in the dark and the cold."
   "The wind sounded frightened."

   What do the sentences mean? Does the wind have feelings? *(No the wind does not have feelings, but the author here uses personification to describe it. Personification is giving human characteristics to an inanimate object. The wind makes an eerie, haunting sound.)*

Supplementary Activities

1. Pa told about his feelings when he saw the "bear" in his way, "My scalp prickled, and my hair stood straight up." (page 111) Have you ever been frightened? In a short paragraph, describe your feelings.

2. Sometimes we laugh when a scary time is over. Ma laughed after she and Laura were safe in the house. Make up another incident when Ma could have laughed the same way, after a frightening incident.

3. Write a letter from Laura and her family to the cousins to tell about the winter.

4. Write an opinion of why the title is good. Suggest another title for the book.

Chapter 7: "The Sugar Snow"   Pages 117-130

Plot Summary
Sugar snow meant an increased yield of maple syrup.

Vocabulary

eaves 117   snuggle 118   troughs 121   delaine 128

basque 128

Discussion Questions and Activities

1. What was sugar snow? *(It was snow in early spring which meant that more maple syrup could be gathered because the late cold snap held the leafing of the trees.)*

2. Have you ever tasted maple syrup? What are the steps in gathering maple syrup? *(bore a hole in a maple tree, hammer trough into the hole, set a cedar bucket on the ground under the flat end of the trough, and collect sap from buckets)*

3. What additional steps are needed to get maple sugar? *(empty sap into a kettle on a bonfire, keep sap boiling, skim every few minutes, boil until sap grains when cooled on a saucer, ladle sap into milk pans)*

4. Look back to the description of whittling the sugar maple troughs. Could you understand only from the narrative? How did the illustration help your understanding?

Supplementary Activities

1. Compare evening entertainment today with the activities in *Little House in the Big Woods*.

Now	Then
•*Homework*	•*Listening to stories*
•*Television*	•*Listening to Pa play the fiddle*
•*Teams—soccer, etc.*	

2. What are some ways to sweeten foods? What are their advantages and disadvantages?

	Advantages	Disadvantages
Maple Sugar:		
Cane Sugar:		
Nutrasweet:		
Corn Syrup:		

3. Why did the Ingalls prefer cane sugar for guests?

Chapter 8: "Dance at Grandpa's"   Pages 131-155

Plot Summary
After helping collect the maple syrup at Grandpa's, the whole Ingalls clan enjoy a party and dance.

Vocabulary

hewed 134	clove-apple 135	yokes 136	swagger 136
bugle 137	napes 138	corsets 140	sprigged 140
flounced 142	pigeon wing 148	jigging 148	

Discussion Questions and Activities

1. What interesting pictures (views) did Laura see on the way to Grandpa's house? *(yellow light of the morning sun, shadows, tracks of wild creatures in the snow)*

2. What were some of the intriguing smells at Grandpa's house at maple sugar time? *(spicy and sweet kitchen smells, hickory logs, clove-apple)* Can you remember any interesting smells from a special place in your childhood (maybe a grandparent's home)? Share the smells for a class brainstorming list. Choose two or three of the sense words to use in a paragraph.

3. Who was Uncle George? Why was he an interesting character? Record your answers about Uncle George on an attribute web.

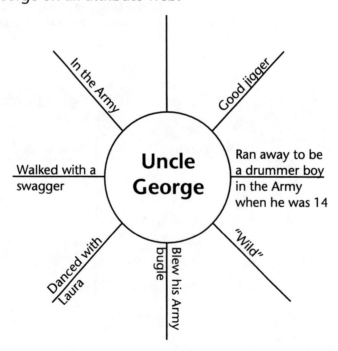

4. What did they do at the dance? *(square dancing, jigging, ate food, made maple sugar candy)* How was the party in the book similar to parties today? How was it different?

Same	Different
•Laughing •Food	•Everyone stayed overnight •No recorded music—live fiddling only

5. Why was the jigging especially fun? *(Grandma and Uncle George had a challenge.)*

Supplementary Activities
1. In music or gym time, try square dancing or listening to a record of some of the songs in the book.

2. Taste some maple syrup or maple syrup candy. Describe its taste in a short paragraph.

3. Writing: Why are parties special?

4. Explain what kind of a movie the book would make. Who would be in the movie? Why?

Chapter 9: "Going to Town"   Pages 156-176

Plot Summary
The Ingalls go to town for supplies. The trip is a special adventure.

Vocabulary
grassflowers 156	pigpen 158	fawn 159	muzzle 159
snarls 161	curried 162	calicos 168	galluses 170
unrumpled 175			

Discussion Questions and Activities
1. What was special about spring for Laura? *(The birds sang, the hazel bushes leafed, the woods were filled with wildflowers, grasshoppers were everywhere, and when it was warm, they ran barefoot.)* What signs of spring do you notice? How is *your* list similar to Laura's?

2. How did Laura and Mary get ready for the trip to town? *(They bathed, curled their hair on rags, and dressed in their best dresses.)*

3. How did Laura describe her hair? *(page 161, dirt-colored brown)* Do you think she was jealous of Mary's golden hair? Why?

4. Describe the store. *(pages 167-168)* Make a list of the things in the store. Use the narrative as well as the illustration. Then sort them into categories. Use your creativity to make categories, the more unusual the better. *(uses, who buys the item, what the item is made of, size)*

5. How did tearing the pocket in her dress make Laura compare herself to Mary? *(Such things never happened to Mary. Laura did not think it was fair.)* Have you ever known anyone who didn't compare well to a brother or sister? How do you think it made them feel? Answer in a few short sentences.

6. What did the lines from Pa's song at the end of the chapter mean? *(Home was a special, safe, comfortable place.)*

Supplementary Activities
1. Classifying: Continue the category game from the store. Students can make lists of possible store items for other classmates to put into categories.

2. Listen in the novel and in other reading for "sound words." Then make up stories using the sound words. Examples might be sounds you like, morning sounds, evening sounds, sounds at the supper table, winter sounds, television sounds, and sounds on the playground.

3. Read poems with word patterns in them and ask students to listen for them. Look in the novel for word patterns. Discuss why authors use word patterns in stories.

4. Listen to a recording or read aloud a portion of the book with vivid descriptions. Ask students to picture in their minds what they are hearing.

5. Have a panel discussion with class members as panelists on how to be a good listener.

6. What does "home" mean? Discuss with a partner. Record your answers on an attribute web. (See next page of this guide.)

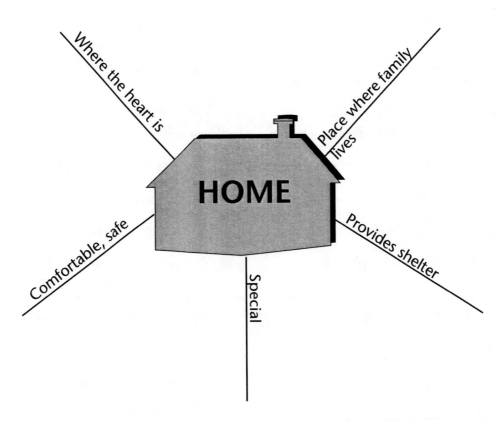

Where the heart is
Place where family lives
Comfortable, safe
HOME
Provides shelter
Special

Chapter 10: "Summertime"   **Pages 177-198**

Plot Summary
Summertime means visitors and a lot of hard work putting up food for the rest of the year.

Vocabulary

gilt 180	primly 181	dreadfully 181	naughty 182
sulked 184	rennet 186	whey 188	sprouts 193

Discussion Questions and Activities

1. What was special about summertime in the little house in the Big Woods? *(Other people came to visit. The weather was warm and pleasant. The children could play outside.)* Why were visitors so special to Laura? *(They were people to see and play with.)*

2. How did Pa satisfy Laura about her brown hair? *(Page 184, He said, "Well, Laura, my hair is brown.")* Why was that a good way to calm Laura? Do parents need to be wise to take care of their children's worries? Think of an example of wise parenting and write a short paragraph about it.

3. What were Ma's steps in making cheese? *(pages 187-188)*

4. How did the bear help Pa find the honey tree? *(The bear was getting honey for himself.)* What were some examples of the plants and animals helping settlers? *(watch dog, animal tracks going toward water, small animals warning about predators)*

Supplementary Activities

1. Research: How do bees make honey? Are there different kinds of honey?

2. Writing: Describe your life in summertime. How is it different from Laura's summer?

3. Analyzing: Who is the main character in the book? How do you know?

4. Analyze the cookie dilemma on page 178 as a math problem.

Chapter 11: "Harvest"   Pages 199-211

Plot Summary
Pa and Uncle Henry work together at harvest time. The reader meets Laura's cousin.

Vocabulary

cradle 200	shocked 202	whetstone 204	sullen 204
tanned 205	steeped 209	horrified 210	monstrously 211

Discussion Questions and Activities

1. Why did Pa and Uncle Henry trade work? *(efficiency, help needed when crops were ripe)*

2. What kind of a person was Charley? Record your answers on an attribute web.

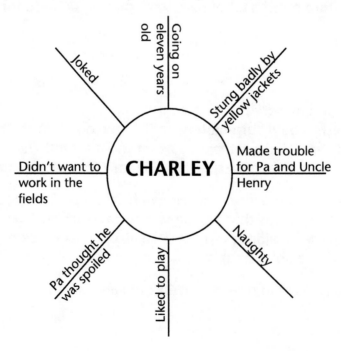

3. Reread the last paragraph of the chapter. Do you understand how Charley could be a liar? Explain.

Supplementary Activities
1. Words with Multiple Meanings: Look in the book for examples of words used in new and different ways from the uses you know; for example, cradle, shock. Make a list of the words with the new meanings and the more familiar meanings. Do the meanings have anything in common?

2. Interview parents or other adults about how much work can be expected of eleven-year-olds. Compare the answers with your classmates.

Chapter 12: "The Wonderful Machine"   Pages 212-228

Plot Summary
The Ingalls life in fall included processing pumpkin and squash, making straw hats, and threshing the wheat.

Vocabulary
sumac 215	hazelnuts 215	hulls 215	separator 222
tumbling rod 222	racket 223	threshers 227	

Discussion Questions and Activities
1. How did Ma make hats? *(She first made many yards of straw braid. Then she soaked the braid in water and shaped a hat, using strong white thread to sew the hat together. When the brim suited her, Ma cut the braid and sewed the end fast.)*

2. How was Laura like the squirrels in the fall? *(She scampered and chattered and collected nuts and acorns.)*

3. Who were the threshers? *(They were men with a threshing machine who went from farm to farm to thresh the wheat.)*

4. Why do you think Pa said the thresher was a great invention? *(It was much faster than hand threshing.)* Ask your parents to tell you about a "great invention" that has made their life easier. Make a class list of great inventions. Choose one for a short report to share with the class. Find out **why** a certain wonderful machine is a great invention.

Supplementary Activities
1. Order: There are many systematic orderly things that the Ingalls do in the book; for example, making cheese, making maple sugar, smoking meat, and making hulled corn. Choose an activity and make a list of the steps on sentence strips. Then put your strips together in an envelope for a classmate to put in order. Check your order by looking back in the book.

2. Each season is special in the Big Woods. Prepare a web to summarize autumn.

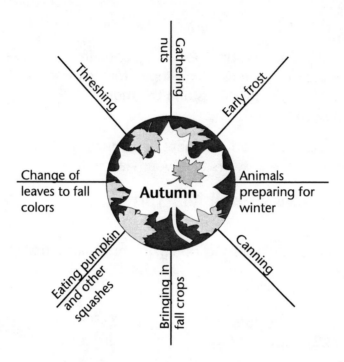

3. Discuss canning and "putting up" the garden vegetables with parents or grandparents.

4. What was the significance of time to the Ingalls? Did they need watches and alarm clocks?

Chapter 13: "The Deer In the Wood" Pages 229-238

Plot Summary:
The Ingalls make preparations for winter. Pa passes on shooting a doe and her fawn.

Vocabulary:

withered 229   deer-lick 230   banking 231   venison 233
grubs 233   waddling 235

Discussion Questions and Activities:
1. How did Pa bank the little house? *(by piling up dead leaves and straw held down by stones to keep out the cold)*

2. Why didn't Pa shoot the fawn? *(He couldn't shoot the deer because he was so beautiful and looked so strong and free and wild.)*

28

3. What was the feeling at the end of the book? *(cozy)*

Culminating Activities

1. Prepare a timeline for the story. The time covered is about a year.

2. Prepare webs for each of the seasons in the book.

3. Higher Order Thinking and Writing: How would the story be different if Laura had a brother?

4. Fill in a story map to summarize the story. (See page 30 of this guide.)

5. Make-up a setting and problem for another story map. Create a class story.

6. Celebrate your learning and enjoyment of the book in one of the following ways:

   • Complete a sociogram to explore Laura's relationships with the other characters in the book. (See page 31 of this guide.)

   • Create a game to review the action in the story. A game board is provided on page 32 as one possibility, but feel free to be creative in adapting any game you enjoy to the story.

   • Write Who's Who entries for three characters from the book.

   • Devise a diary for one of the book's characters.

   • Speculation on the future for the Ingalls Family.

Story Map

```
   ╭─────────────╮
   │   Setting   │
   ╰─────────────╯
          │
          ▼
   ╭─────────────╮
   │   Problem   │
   ╰─────────────╯
          │
          ▼
   ╭─────────────╮
   │    Goal     │
   ╰─────────────╯
          │
          ▼
   ╭─────────────╮
   │  Episodes   │
   ╰─────────────╯
          │
          ▼
   ╭─────────────╮
   │ Resolution  │
   ╰─────────────╯
```

Characters_____

_____

_____

_____

Time and Place_____

_____

_____

_____

_____

Beginning ———→ Development ———→ Outcome

_____

_____

_____

_____

_____

_____

_____

_____

_____

Laura's Relationship with the Other Characters in the Book

Directions: In the circles surrounding Laura, list the other characters in the book. On the arrows provide a word or phrase to describe the relationship. Be sure to describe the relationship going both ways; e.g., Laura to Pa as well as Pa to Laura.

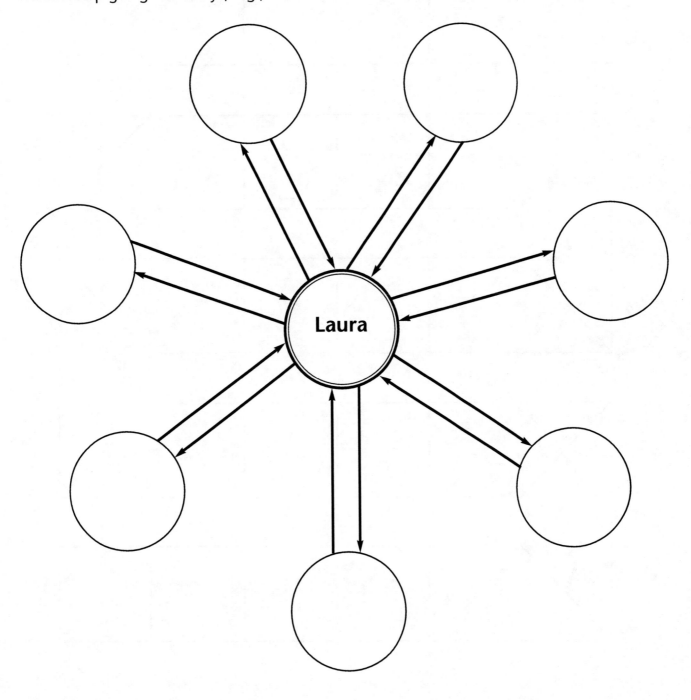

31

Novel Units Game Board

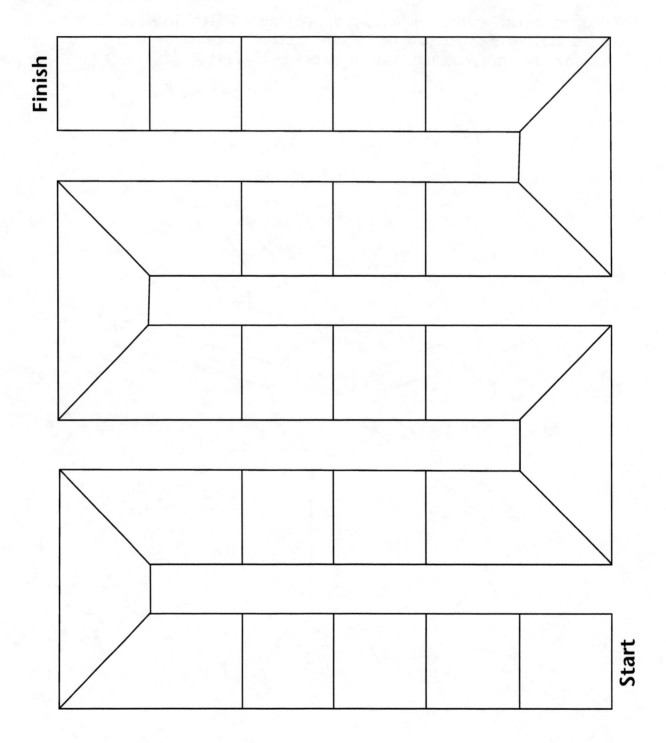

Little House Celebration

Stage a Little House Celebration for a day or part of a day.

1. Divide the class into groups of 5 or 6 to take the parts of the Wilder Family; Pa, Ma, Laura, Mary, Carrie, and Jack.

2. Prepare signs for any inventions in your classroom not yet invented 100 years ago.

3. Decorate the classroom in a Little House scenario.

4. Collect games that would have been played in the little house. Remember that you can create some new games.

5. Research food for the celebration. (See Chapter 4 and *The Little House Cookbook*.)

6. Look for pictures of the various animals and plants mentioned in the book. Add short paragraphs of information about each.

© Novel Units, Inc.

33

Art Projects

1. Prepare an architect's floor plan of the little house in the Big Woods.

2. Make frost and snowflake pictures by folding white paper into fourths and cutting an interesting design.

3. Draw a picture of Laura's Christmas rag doll.

4. Draw the panels for a cartoon explaining some of the things the Ingalls do. (cleaning the gun, churning butter, smoking a pig, etc.)

5. Picture in your mind Pa's Christmas present for Ma. Then draw a picture of it.

6. Draw a picture of Ma in her fancy dress. (page 128)

7. Using pieces of fabric, cut out pioneer dresses. Attach the dress to paper figures.

8. Using white paper like snow, draw some tracks of wild creatures that Laura might have seen.

9. In Chapter 12, Ma made straw hats. Try to braid with straw or some long grassy weeds that you can find.

10. Investigate Garth Williams, the illustrator of the book.

11. Make some drawings in the style of Garth Williams.

12. Create a photo album belonging to a character in the book. Provide appropriate captions.

Bibliography of Teacher References

Little House Country: Photo Guide to the Home States of Laura Ingalls Wilder. Terrell Publishing, Inc., Kansas City, MO 64120

Laura Ingalls Wilder Memorial Society, Pepin, Wisconsin 54759

Little House on the Prairie, Inc., Independence, Kansas 67301

Franklin County Historical Society, Malone, NY 12953

Laura Ingalls Wilder Tourist Center, Walnut Grove, Minnesota 56180

Laura Ingalls Wilder Park and Museum, Burr Oak, Iowa 52131

Laura Ingalls Wilder Memorial Society, DeSmet, South Dakota 57231

Laura Ingalls Wilder Home and Museum, Mansfield, Missouri 65704

Assessment for *Little House in the Big Woods*

Overview: Assessment is an on-going process. The following ten items can be completed during the novel study. Both teacher and student check them. Points may be added to indicate the level of understanding.

Name _____ Date _____

Student   **Teacher**

_____   _____   1. Keep a predicting chart as you read the book.

_____   _____   2. Interact with the vocabulary words using 2 or 3 of the activities from pages 4 and 5.

_____   _____   3. Keep a journal while you read the book. (See writing ideas on page 6.)

_____   _____   4. Compare your life to that of the Ingalls. Use a T-diagram, Venn, or illustration to report.

_____   _____   5. Complete an attribute web for one of the book's characters.

_____   _____   6. Present a Reader's Theater for a favorite incident in the book.

_____   _____   7. Summarize the book with a complete story map.

_____   _____   8. Choose one of the culminating activities to complete with a partner.

_____   _____   9. Stage a *Little House Celebration* (page 33) and then write a short paragraph describing the event.

_____   _____   10. Write a letter to a friend describing the study of the book. Be sure to include your evaluation of the book.